How to Get Rid of Self-Doubt and Start Believing in Yourself

An Essential Guide to Developing Self-Confidence and Boosting Self-Esteem

by Alexi Weaver

Table of Contents

Introduction 1

Chapter 1: Empowering Yourself with a Positive Mindset 7

Chapter 2: Managing Your Emotions Effectively 13

Chapter 3: Improving Yourself from the Outside ... 19

Chapter 4: Transforming Yourself from the Inside . 25

Chapter 5: How Learning Impacts Self-Esteem and Self-Confidence 31

Conclusion 35

Introduction

Rate your self-confidence on a scale of 1 to 10, with 1 being the lowest and 10 being the highest. Done? Good. Next, rate your self-esteem on the same scale. Confused? This is not a trick question. It's a common misconception that self-confidence and self-esteem mean the same thing and that the two words can be used interchangeably. However, there are significant differences between self-confidence and self-esteem.

I'll explain:

Self-confidence is often the result of learning and achievement. When we are able to overcome a certain obstacle, our level of self-confidence increases. Likewise, it also grows when we are able to improve or learn a skill.

For you to have a clear picture of what confidence is, let us take the example of an aspiring singer named Joe. He is about to enter into a regional competition and he has been preparing for the past six months. Having gone through rigorous training with a competent mentor, he is highly confident that he has a good shot at winning the contest. From Joe's example we can see that because he has honed his skill in singing, his level of confidence has increased.

On the other hand, self-esteem has more to do with how we perceive ourselves in the eyes of others. It is significantly affected by social norms imposed by the society that surrounds us. Generally, people who have a high sense of self-esteem are comfortable and happy with themselves. They like what they see in the mirror and they do not let other people treat them poorly. They know exactly what they're worth and they don't settle for less.

To understand self-esteem further, let us look into the life of a young teenager named Christine. Because of puberty, she suffered from severe acne. Luckily, with medication and a thorough skin regimen, Christine's acne problem subsided. Her face became clearer and, most importantly, she started to feel good about herself. Before, her acne got in the way of interacting with other people. Her insecurities made her shy around her peers. As her skin problem disappeared, Christine has started to socialize more. She successfully made new friends and is finally living her life like a normal teenager. Her self-esteem has clearly improved and along with it, her quality of life.

Even though self-confidence and self-esteem are different, they are equally important. When you lack either one, or both, your life is severely restrained by a sense of self-doubt which only further hinders you from self-improvement and from connecting with others.

If you are currently living in self-doubt, a victim of your own insecurities, now is the time to free yourself from its shackles and unlock the hidden potential within you. With this book, you will learn to believe in yourself and feel confident about what you have to offer. It will take you on a step-by-step process to develop your self-confidence and boost your self-esteem. So if you're ready to take back control over your life, then let's get started!

© Copyright 2015 by Miafn LLC - All rights reserved.

This document is geared towards providing reliable information in regards to the topic and issue covered. The publication is sold with the idea that the publisher is not required to render accounting, officially permitted, or otherwise, qualified services. If advice is necessary, legal or professional, a practiced individual in the profession should be ordered.

- From a Declaration of Principles which was accepted and approved equally by a Committee of the American Bar Association and a Committee of Publishers and Associations.

In no way is it legal to reproduce, duplicate, or transmit any part of this document in either electronic means or in printed format. Recording of this publication is strictly prohibited and any storage of this document is not allowed unless with written permission from the publisher. All rights reserved.

The information provided herein is stated to be truthful and consistent, in that any liability, in terms of inattention or otherwise, by any usage or abuse of any policies, processes, or directions contained within is solely and completely the responsibility of the recipient reader. Under no circumstances will any legal responsibility or blame be held against the publisher for any reparation, damages, or monetary loss due to the information herein, either directly or indirectly.

Respective authors own all copyrights not held by the publisher.

The information herein is offered for informational purposes solely, and is universal as so. The presentation of the information is without contract or any type of guarantee assurance.

The trademarks that are used are without any consent, and the publication of the trademark is without permission or backing by the trademark owner. All trademarks and brands within this book are for clarifying purposes only and are the owned by the owners themselves, not affiliated with this document.

Chapter 1: Empowering Yourself with a Positive Mindset

People who suffer from low self-esteem and low self-confidence have negative mindsets. They are pessimists who expect nothing but the worst from everything and everyone. Likewise, their focus is only set on mistakes, and this prevents them from seeing even the most significant achievements. Most of the time, their minds are filled with negative thoughts about themselves. "I am going to fail this job." "I am not good enough for this person."

If you have this mindset, you need to take action to replace it with a positive one. Everything begins from the mind, including change. So, if you want to alter your life, you have to start with your mindset. Here are several ways that you can try to help you cultivate a positive mindset:

Identify Your Negative Thoughts

The most important step in cultivating a positive mindset is to identify your negative thoughts first. Your negative thoughts may sound similar to these: "I am not beautiful enough." "I am fat." "I am not smart enough for this task." "I am a complete failure." "I am not as good at this as other people." Sounds familiar?

Take a piece of paper and list these thoughts. As you create this list, be honest with yourself. Write everything down and do not make the mistake of justifying your negative thoughts. When you are done, read your completed list and take note of every single thought that you have identified. This is for you to easily identify these thoughts the next time that they surface in your mind.

Recording your negative thoughts also develops your mindfulness. Seeing all the negative thoughts that you have cultivated inside your head will give you a true sense of how much negativity you have been subjecting yourself to. Becoming aware of this will open up your mind to realities that you have been blind to before.

There are two ways to finish this exercise, each with their own unique benefits. First, you can choose to keep this list somewhere private; in a private drawer perhaps or in a safety deposit box, if you have one. Do not read it again until you have completed your improvement. When you deem that your self-esteem and self-confidence are already high, take out your list and read it to yourself. You will be surprised and empowered by the transformation that you have made. It will strengthen you and remind you of how much you have improved.

On the other hand, you can choose to destroy this list. Tear it apart, burn it, whichever way you like. This gesture will be a symbol of you letting go of the negativity that you have held on to for so long. Many find this act freeing and surely you will too.

Change Your Negative Thoughts to Positive Thoughts

Changing your negative thoughts into positive ones is difficult but not impossible to do. It only requires two things: willpower and determination. To turn your negativity into positivity, you should acknowledge it as it surfaces inside your mind. Recognize that it is a negative thought and that you should do something about it. Next, "twist" the way you think. Inside your head, make the negative statement into a positive one. For example, imagine yourself handling a big project at work. Because of your low self-esteem and self-confidence, you tell yourself: "I am not capable of doing this. I should pass this project over to someone else more competent than I am." As this thought enters your head, quickly change it into a positive statement. "Twist" it into something like: "This is a challenging project but I can do this. All I need to do is to carefully plan this out so I won't mess it up."

Then put your positive thought into action. Take it one step at a time.

Doing this for the first few times might be hard, but as you continue to "twist" your negative thoughts into positive ones, it will become a habit. Soon, you will find yourself thinking only of positivity.

Surround Yourself with a Strong Support System

In several studies, psychologists have determined that children who are constantly brought down by their own parents are least likely to succeed. They also develop emotional problems later on in life. From this we can learn that the people who surround us affect our self-esteem and self-confidence. This is not only applicable to our family but also to our friends, workmates, or classmates.

When we are surrounded by people who have self-esteem and self-confidence issues themselves, we are "infected" by their negativity. Because they are insecure, they take it out on other people. They prey on the mistakes of others and they have a criticism for almost everything and everyone. They will pick on you and make sure that you stay at the bottom with them.

Avoid these people as much as possible. If your friends are a threat to your self-esteem and self-confidence, then change your circle. Surround yourself with friends who lift you up and encourage you to be the best you. However, there are some instances wherein you cannot avoid these people most especially if they are your immediate family. If this is the case, just you have two options: either block them out or take their negativity as a driving force for you to improve yourself.

Blocking these people out can be tricky, especially if you eat at the same dinner table. You don't want to be impolite either. What you can do is just pretend that you are listening to them when in fact, you really aren't. When they attack you with their negativity, fill your mind with positive thoughts. It will be difficult at first but eventually, you will get the hang of it.

Another way to deal with this is to use their negative statements as a source of motivation. For example, if a parent calls you an "idiot," do not let it get to your head. Instead, assure yourself that you are not one. Tell yourself you are not an "idiot" and that you are going to prove it to yourself. Not to them, but to yourself.

Chapter 2: Managing Your Emotions Effectively

Frustrations and insecurities are magnified because of your emotions. They create unnecessary stress and make your issues seem bigger than they actually are. To avoid these, you have to manage your emotions effectively. Our emotions are difficult to control, but by developing positive habits, we can prevent them from taking over.

Have Patience with Yourself

Recovering from low self-esteem and self-confidence is a long and winding journey. It does not happen overnight so be patient with yourself. As you work on improving yourself, there will be times when you will feel impatient. You might start to think that you are not making any progress because your improvement is taking too long. Do not entertain these negative thoughts. Instead, when these thoughts surface inside your mind, you can "twist" them into positive ones or you can use meditation to restore your mind's balance.

The moment you feel that your emotions are getting out of hand, take some time off from what you are doing. Whether you are at work or at home, remove yourself from the task at hand and find a place conducive for meditation. It can be your bedroom or any vacant room in your office building where you are free from distraction.

Next, take a seat on any surface. If there is a chair where you can comfortably recline your back then that would be ideal. If there is none available, you can position yourself in a sitting position on the floor. Close your eyes and bring yourself to a state of relaxation. Clearing your mind from strong emotions might take some time, so be patient with this process. Just focus on your breathing. Inhale through your nose and exhale through your mouth. Continue to regularize your breathing throughout your meditation.

When you already feel relaxed, utter this or a similar mantra: "I am in control." Continue your breathing for another minute and as you breathe, concentrate on your mantra. Internalize it. Repeat this process three times. When finished, slowly come to your awareness and open your eyes. You should feel relaxed and calm after you have finished this meditation.

Stop Thinking That Others Are Better Than You

A habit that people with low self-esteem and self-confidence have is thinking that they are inferior to other people. They constantly put themselves down by comparing themselves with others. "I am not as beautiful as (insert name here)." "He is more intelligent than I am." If you have this habit, break yourself free from it. You are not doing yourself any favor by thinking that others are better than you.

When you are tempted to compare yourself to others, remind yourself of this thought: no one is above the other. We are only born different. Contrary to what you believe in, no one was made better and "more special" than the others. We just have a different set of talents and skills compared to others.

"But I don't have any talents and skills!" Yes, you do. You are just too engrossed in seeing the best in others that you fail to see the best in you. If you feel this way, take a piece of pen and paper and list down your talents and skills.

"I can't sing. I can't dance. I can't write. I can't draw. I don't have any talents or skills to list down." Yes, you do. You have unique talents and skills within you. They may not be of the musical or literary kind. You see, there are other kinds of talents and skills, too, and they are as useful and quite practical. Managing a household effectively, listening to others, making others laugh and being able to give a sound advice to others are talents and skills, too.

As you create your list, think of the unique characteristics that you have. Can you make friends easily? Can you follow instructions to the letter? Can you convince others easily? Write these talents and skills down. Write as many as you can and when you're finished, take a look at the list that you have made. Realize that you too have talents and skills that others might not possess. Keep this list in a place where you can see it often. You can paste it on your desk or keep it on the front page of your daily planner. It will serve as your reminder each time you start to question yourself again.

Learn from Your Mistakes

In the past, you might have fed your low self-esteem and self-confidence by dwelling on your mistakes. Now is the time to break that habit. Each time that you commit a mistake, refuse from focusing on it and instead, learn from it. Mistakes are normal in life so stop being a perfectionist. Without mistakes, we will never learn valuable lessons.

Learning from your mistakes requires a higher level of understanding which you can develop through constant practice. Whenever you commit a mistake, surely criticism follows. It can come from others or it can come from yourself. When you are faced with a criticism, take it positively.

For example, in the workplace, we usually deal with criticisms from our superiors. When you are being verbally reprimanded or criticized for a mistake that you have made, just keep silent and when they are done, show them your appreciation. Be sure to express it sincerely and in a professional manner as there is a risk that they might think you are being sarcastic. You can simply tell your superiors, "Thank you, Sir. I appreciate your criticism and I will put it in mind the next time I am faced with a similar task." Recognize that you cannot take back what you have done. The only thing that you can do is to do better the next time around.

Chapter 3: Improving Yourself from the Outside

Most of the insecurities that people with low self-esteem and self-confidence deal with stem from their physical appearance. They go about life comparing how they look with other people in their surroundings. In the workplace, they compare themselves to the "smart-looking and gorgeous" co-worker. In the family, they compare themselves to the "better-looking" sibling.

If you have found yourself entertaining these thoughts, snap out of it. Stop comparing the way you look with others. Same as with our talents and skills, each of us is born with a unique physical appearance. What you can see in the mirror is a product of your parent's genes. It is not because you got "unlucky" or "cursed." You are beautifully made, no matter how you look. Each part of you, from your hair down to your toes are from your wonderful parents. The next time that you feel "ugly" or "displeasing", remind yourself of this fact.

Perhaps you have already thought of cosmetic surgery and have been discouraged about how expensive it is. Well, there are more affordable ways to improve your physical appearance without having to spend a lot of money and without changing the beautiful physical features that you have been born with. With proper hygiene and by wearing the right clothes, you can significantly improve your physical appearance.

Observing Proper Hygiene

You have been taught this lesson since you were a kid. Proper hygiene involves cleaning up after your body by regularly taking a bath, brushing your teeth and seeing professionals which can aide in your routine. For example, to make sure that your skin is clear, you can see a dermatologist who can give you sound medical advice on what regimen works well for your skin. Your dermatologist will first assess your skin type before making his recommendations. For your dental hygiene, you need to see a dental hygienist regularly too. Brushing your teeth is not enough to maintain proper dental hygiene. You need to get regular cleanings if you want to avoid annoying problems such as bad breath.

Proper hygiene does not only limit itself to how we take care of our physical bodies. It also involves our day to day actions and surroundings. Too often, when we are busy, we don't mind making a mess but proper hygiene calls for us to practice discipline and cleanliness as we do our daily activities. Furthermore, proper hygiene also dictates that we should keep our surroundings clean. Take a look around you. Is your home orderly? Is everything in its right place and is the trash properly disposed of? If yes, then that is good. You have already crossed one off the proper hygiene list. However, if your answer is no, it's time to clean it up.

You might be wondering how proper hygiene is related to your self-esteem and self-confidence: "How can keeping myself and my surroundings clean and proper help me improve my self-esteem and self-confidence?" You will be surprised at the significant improvement this step will cause in your life. Even if this step does not involve physically altering your appearance, it makes you and your home presentable to others. You will start to feel more confident because you know that you have already cleaned up well.

Wearing the Right Clothes

Wearing the right clothes can effectively boost your self-esteem and self-confidence. You don't need a lot of money for this. All you need in this step is research and creativity. In the past, you might have invested a lot of money in signature clothing. What you have done was completely normal. You were trying to compensate with expensive clothing believing that it can make you look better but you will not make that same mistake again. This time, you are going to do some responsible shopping by making sure that your money goes to all clothes that flatter your body and personality.

Before hitting the racks, the first thing that you need to do is to identify your body type. Each of us has a unique body structure which fashion gurus label according to their shapes. You have probably heard some of the common terms that they use. For example, to describe a body structure with equal bust and bottom measurements and a well-defined waist, they use the term "hour glass" type.

To get started, look for a list of different body types. There are numerous online and printed sources that you can access for free. When you have already acquired a list, the next thing that you need to do is to take your own measurements. If you have a friend or a relative who is willing to help you with this step, then you can ask them to take your measurements for you. Having someone else to take your measurements proves to be more convenient and accurate. Using a measuring tape, first take a measurement of your bust. Next, take a measurement of your waist and finally, your hips. Note these three measurements down on a list of paper and compare them to the list that you previously researched. Match your measurements with the body type that it best corresponds with. Once you have already determined what type of body shape you have, it's time to do some research on what kind of clothes will best flatter you.

With your body shape in mind, make a research on what kind of clothes will compliment your structure. You cannot just go into stores and select clothes with colors and cuts that you like. At this point, it is important for you to shop for useful clothes which will help you improve your self-esteem and self-confidence.

There are a specific set of clothes for each unique body type. For example, for individuals with a body shaped like an inverted triangle, halter tops will look good on them. This specific cut softens out their wide shoulders giving them a softer and a balanced look. For you to be aware of what kind of clothes will best flatter your structure, make a research on it by reading through printed or online sources. Fashion magazines contain informative articles which you will find helpful and there are thousands of articles online which you can access for free.

Chapter 4: Transforming Yourself from the Inside

Another way of taking care of yourself is to care for your body from the inside. You can do this by leading a healthy lifestyle. Choosing to adopt healthy habits comes with numerous benefits. If you are insecure about your body, exercise and sports can help you achieve your weight goals. If you are insecure about your health, proper dieting and getting enough rest can help you overcome your health issues.

The Wonders of Exercise

Exercise can do wonders for your self-esteem. With regular exercise, you will look good and feel good. First, let us start with the looking good part. As mentioned earlier, your insecurities might stem from your physical appearance. Although exercise will not change your facial features, it can give you a toned body and clearer skin. You can also put on or reduce weight with it. However, exercise does not only work on the outside. Regular exercise most especially cardio activities stimulate feel good hormones which helps you fight anxiousness and other negative emotions related to self-esteem and self-confidence. Enrolling yourself in a physical fitness gym also gives you the opportunity to interact with others, helping you deal with your anti-social behavior. It's a great leap but will ultimately be one of the best decisions that you will ever make.

Getting regular exercise is easy as long as you commit to it. It won't take a lot of your time so do not make a pass by saying that you are too busy for it. Ideally, it would be great if you can exercise daily. To do so, all you have to do is set aside a few minutes of your day to perform exercise routines. There are many exercise routines on YouTube that you can follow. Some of them will only take as little as 15 minutes of your time.

The best time to perform your quick exercise routine can either be at the start of your day or at the end of your day. You can do it also inside your bedroom, outside on your backyard or in any available space that you have in your home. During this time, set aside all the chores and tasks that you need to do. If you have children, ask them not to disturb you during this time. If you have already memorized the exercise routine, you can start on your own. However, if you still need a guide, you can follow a video on a monitor screen or even on your own tablet device.

If you have extra hours to spare and you want to try out something new, enrolling yourself in a physical fitness gym is a great idea! With the help of a certified fitness professional, you will be given a specific program made especially for your body's needs. Likewise, you will meet a lot of new faces as you work out. This can help you break out of your anti-social behavior. With a common topic to talk about (physical fitness or fitness goals) you can easily make friends so do not hesitate to make some when you enroll!

The Necessity of a Proper Diet

Another important aspect of your new, healthy lifestyle is your personal diet. What you eat does not only affect you physically. It also affects you emotionally. Unhealthy food can be bad for your hormones and that will only make your self-esteem and self-confidence issues worse.

If you have a fitness goal (if you want to lose or gain weight), you can go on a special diet as advised by a dietician. Although there are many diet sources readily available on the internet and on printed media, it is best to seek advice from a medical professional who can create a specific diet program for you. You must understand that each one of us has unique body functions so there is no "one-size-fits-all" diet.

If you simply want to adopt a healthier way of eating, just remember your childhood lessons on what a balanced diet is. To remind you, a balanced diet consists of the right amount of essential nutrients and minerals that the human body needs. Apply this balanced way of eating in all your meals and try to avoid processed and oily food. That means you have to say goodbye to your fast food meals as they can be very dangerous to your body.

The Importance of Sleep

Many neglect the importance of sleep, not realizing that it has a very powerful effect on one's overall wellness. Having enough sleep keeps us alert all throughout the day. It also promotes the healthy function of our internal organs and regulates our hormones. There are many people who will convince you that six hours of sleep is already enough but it's always best to go back to the basics. Remember when your mother or primary school teacher taught you that eight hours of sleep is the ideal number? It still is. Even if you have outgrown your teddy bear pajamas, your body still needs the same amount of sleep.

Chapter 5: How Learning Impacts Self-Esteem and Self-Confidence

Without the proper education, an individual can feel unprepared and incapable of handling tasks and jobs entrusted to him. When a person feels inadequacy he starts to doubt himself. He starts thinking, "Maybe I'm not smart enough." "They should give this task/job to someone more capable." These negative thoughts then feed on his self-esteem and self-confidence. If this situation happened to you in the past, know that with proper education you can do anything that you desire to. Proper education doesn't require you to get a university degree. After all, there are many other ways of increasing your knowledge aside from attending formal classroom instructions.

Join Skill-Building Clubs

There are many skill-building clubs available in your community. You can acquire a list of them by browsing online or by asking your friends, co-workers or relatives. These clubs serve as excellent venues for acquiring skills that will not only add to your skill set but will also improve your self-esteem and self-confidence. If you cannot decide on which club to join, the best club that you could participate in is a speaking club. International organizations such as The Toastmaster's Club have branches in almost every town or city all over the world. By joining these speaking clubs, you do not only enhance your speaking skills but you also learn different strategies to break out of your shell.

Avail of Online Training Courses

This is ideal for people whose are pressed for time. Despite your busy schedule, you can further your education with the help of modern technology. By taking an online training course, you get to learn a new skill without compromising your schedule and without spending a lot of money.

Read, Read and Read!

The best way to increase your knowledge is to read. Where else can you find all the essential knowledge in this world? You can find them in books. Cultivate the habit of reading. You can start by sparing 15 minutes of your day reading any book of your choice. It is best to pick a book which has a genre that you are interested in.

Conclusion

Develop this daily habit: when you wake up in the morning, face yourself in the mirror and tell yourself, "You are enough." Stand there for a few more seconds as you internalize this thought. When you say these words, truly mean them. Convince yourself that truly, you are enough. You are beautiful enough. You are smart enough. You are talented or skilled enough. You are enough, because you really are. They say it takes 21 days to build a habit so continue doing this exercise for 21 days. At first, you won't sound so convinced. In time, you will soon realize that what you are telling yourself is true.

You are enough. You just couldn't see it yourself because you have been blinded by your low self-esteem and self-confidence. You are beautifully made and you have so much potential within you. The only person who is standing in the way for you to become the best you is you. So step away from this close quarter situation, look at things from a different perspective, start believing in yourself and watch yourself and your life improve.

Finally, I'd like to thank you for purchasing this book! If you found it helpful, I'd greatly appreciate it if you'd take a moment to leave a review on Amazon. Thank you!

Printed in Great Britain
by Amazon